Gnomologia

A collection of the
proverbs, maxims and adages
that inspired
Benjamin Franklin
and *Poor Richard's Almanack*

1732

Illustrations by Edward Barbini

LEVENGER
PRESS

Published by Levenger Press
420 South Congress Avenue
Delray Beach, Florida 33445 USA
www.Levengerpress.com

This book contains selections from the original *Gnomologia*, compiled
by Thomas Fuller, M. D., and published in London in 1732. The full
title was *Gnomologia: Adagies and Proverbs; Wise Sentences and Witty
Sayings, Ancient and Modern, Foreign and British.*

First Edition

Library of Congress Cataloging-in-Publication Data

Gnomologia. Selections
   Gnomologia : a collection of the proverbs, maxims and adages that
inspired Benjamin Franklin and Poor Richard's almanack / illustrations
by Edward Barbini. -- 1st ed.
         p. cm.
   Includes index.
   "This book contains selections from the original Gnomologia,
compiled by Thomas Fuller, M.D., and published in London in 1732"--
T.p. verso.
   ISBN 978-1-929154-32-6
   1.   Proverbs. 2.   Maxims.   I. Fuller, Thomas, 1654-1734. II.
Barbini., Edward. III. Title.
   PN6403.G662 2008
   398.9'21--dc22
                                                    2008005856

Cover and book design by Danielle Furci
Mim Harrison, Editor

With grateful acknowledgment to

The Library Company OF PHILADELPHIA

Benjamin Franklin, Founder

List of Illustrations

Contents

To the Reader
1732

All of us forget more than we remember, and therefore it hath been my constant Custom to note down and record whatever I thought of my self, or receiv'd from Men, or Books worth preserving.

Among other things, I wrote out Apothegms, Maxims, Proverbs, acute Expressions, vulgar Sayings, &c.

And having at length collected more than ever any *Englishman* has before me, I have ventur'd to send them forth, to try their Fortune among the People.

In ancient Times, before methodical Learning had got Footing in the Nations, and instructive Treatises were written, the Observations that wise Men made from Experience, were us'd to be gather'd and summ'd up into brief and comprehensive Sentences, which being so contriv'd, as to have something remarkable in their Expressions, might be easily remember'd, and brought into Use on Occasions: These are call'd Adagies or Maxims.

Many of these are only plain bare Expressions, to be taken literally in their proper Meaning; others have something of the Obscure and Surprize, which as soon as understood, renders them pretty and notable.

It's a matter of no small Pains and Diligence (whatever lazy, snarling Persons may think) to pick up so many independent Particulars, as I have here done.

To the Reader 1732

And it's no trifling or useless thing neither; it being what many of the most learned and wisest Men in the World, have in all Ages employ'd themselves upon.

–*Thomas Fuller, M.D.*
London

To the Reader
2032

We are taking the liberty of addressing this to the readers of years hence because after discovering this eighteenth-century book among the treasures of the Library Company of Philadelphia, we're quite certain that much of this gnomologia will be around for decades to come. Perhaps even centuries.

Gnomologia, a grand old word rooted in the Greek for "to know," is the title of the collection of maxims, proverbs and aphorisms that Dr. Thomas Fuller of London, England, compiled in 1732. It seems to have been painstaking work that left the good doctor cranky at times. He reminds us in his introduction (from which the 1732 "To the Reader" is excerpted) that he alphabetized the collection "not as any help to the Reader, but to my self, that I might the better avoid Repetitions, which otherwise would be extremely difficult."

But despite his dyspepsia, Dr. Fuller did provide a great help to one Reader in particular: his book became one of the primary sources of material for Benjamin Franklin's *Poor Richard's Almanack*.

An American original...from centuries before

We discovered this fact—and the *Gnomologia* book—at the Library Company of Philadelphia, which Franklin founded in 1731. (It took some digging, which is part of the delight: the title page had actually been pasted over with another page.)

The Library acquired the book in 2005 and with it, was able to complete the puzzle of the various sources that Franklin drew on for his homespun, endearing—and enduring—adages.

> This American original was not all that original in his choice of maxims. But who ever was?

"Franklin," says the writer James Geary (*The Word in a Phrase*, 2005), "is the founding father of the American aphorism." And so there is a certain irony in discovering that this American original was not all that original in his choice of maxims. But who ever was?

Franklin was simply putting his ingenious (and original) stamp on a tradition that even then dated back centuries—to Sir Francis Bacon in the seventeenth century, to Montaigne and Erasmus in the sixteenth, and even earlier to Plutarch. And these are only some of the many written chronicles.

Begged, borrowed, but never stolen

Proverbs predate the pen: they are part of an oral tradition that still beguiles a sophisticated society, knowledge gathered in one age and distilled through many more. Isaac D'Israeli, in his *Curiosities of Literature* (1791), posits that in earlier times these proverbs were probably "the unwritten language of morality." His assessment of "these neglected fragments of wisdom" still works today. They "still offer many interesting objects for the studies of the philosopher and the historian."

Maxims are meant to be borrowed and begged, so they're never really stolen. They are the palimpsest of a wisdom that remains constant in an ever-changing universe.

And thus Benjamin Franklin helped to set the stage for other famous American aphorists such as Mark Twain, Will Rogers and Yogi Berra.

Déjà-vu all over again

The Levenger Press edition of *Gnomologia* represents a selection from Dr. Fuller's prodigious collection. For the most part, we have hewed to his alphabetical presentation.

As a service to the Reader, we have also included an Index of Key Words, to help you more quickly find that saying about the Cat or the Fool.

We expect—in fact, we hope— that you will find some adages so familiar as to startle you with how

> Maxims are the palimpsest of a wisdom that remains constant in an ever-changing universe.

long they've been around. There is also the delight of discovering anew some old sayings that still ring true.

As D'Israeli observed, "Truth and nature can never be obsolete." A certain reassurance comes in knowing that there really is nothing much new under the sun, that there is knowledge we've known for centuries (if temporarily forgotten), and that these wise words may carry on for generations yet.

–Editor, Levenger Press
Delray Beach

The absent Party is still faulty.

After Cheese comes nothing.

After this Leaf another grows.

After Meat, Mustard.

Against the Wild-fire of the Mob there's no Defence.

Age and Wedlock bring a Man to his Night-Cap.

Agree, for the Law is costly.

Always you are to be rich next Year.

Anger is many times more hurtful, than the Injury that caused it.

All...

...Cats are alike grey in the Night.

...Doors open to Courtesy.

...Fish are not caught with Flies.

...is but Lip-Wisdom, that wanteth Experience.

...is not Butter that comes from the Cow.

...is not Gold that glitters.

...is not lost that is in Peril.

...the Joys in the World cannot take one grey Hair out of our Heads.

...Saint without, all Devil within.

...that's said in the Parlour, should not be heard in the Hall.

...things are difficult, before they are easy.

Enquire not what boils in another's Pot.

As...

...a Cat loves Mustard.

...brisk as a Bee in a Tar-Pot.

...demure as if Butter would not melt in his Mouth.

...fit as a Fritter for a Friar's Mouth.

...fit as a Thump with a Stone in an Apothecary's Eye.

...good have no Time, as make no good Use of it.

...high as a Hog, all but the Bristles.

...innocent as a Devil of two Years old.

...irrecoverable as a Lump of Butter in
a Greyhound's Mouth.

...is the Gander, so is the Goose.

...kind as a Kite; all you can't eat, you hide.

...lazy as *Ludlam's* Dog, that lean'd his Head
against the Wall to bark.

...like as two Peas.

...long as I live, I'll spit in my Parlour.

...mad as a *March*-Hare.

...much Wit as three Folks, two Fools and a Madman.

...nimble as a Cow in a Cage.

...useless as Monkey's Grease.

...welcome as Water in a leaking Ship.

...welcome as Water in one's Shoes.

...a Wolf is like a Dog, so is a Flatterer like a Friend.

...you make your Bed, so lie down.

Anger may glance into the Breast of a wise Man –
but rests only in the Bosom of Fools.

The Anvil fears no Blows.

An Angler eats more than he gets.

Any thing for a quiet Life.

Arrogance is a Weed that grows mostly in a Dunghill.

An Ass is but an Ass, tho' laden with Gold.

An Ass was never cut out for a Lap-Dog.

At Court, every one for himself.

At the Gate which Suspicion enters, Love goes out.

Bad Excuses are worse than none.

The Bait hides the Hook.

Bald Heads are soon shaven.

Barbarous Asses ride on *Barbary* Horses.

Bare Words buy no Barley.

Be content; the Sea hath Fish enough.

Be not choleric; 'twill make you look old.

Beauty will buy no Beef.

The Belief and Hope of Heaven, is a sufficient
Encouragement to Virtue, when all others fail.

The Belly hates a long Sermon.

Better...

...be stung by a Nettle, than prick'd by a Rose.

...be up to the Ancles, than quite over Head and Ears.

...cut the Shoe, than pinch the Foot.

...eat Salt with Philosophers of *Greece*, than
eat Sugar with Courtezans of *Italy*.

...the Foot slip, than the Tongue.

...give the Wool than the whole Sheep.

...go to Heaven in Rags, than to Hell in Embroidery.

...keep the Devil at the Door, than turn him
out of the House.

...late than never.

...ride an Ass that carries us, than a Horse
that throws us.

...some of a Pudding than none of a Pye.

...to say here it is, than here it was.

Gnomologia

The best is at the Bottom.

The best Metals lose their Lustre, unless
brightened by Use.

The best Surgeon is he, that has been well
hack'd himself.

Best to bend it while a Twig.

Better's the last Smile, than the first Laughter.

Blind Men's Wives need no Paint.

The Body is the Workhouse of the Soul.

A Book that is shut, is but a Block.

Both Folly and Wisdom come upon us with Years.

The Boughs that bear most, hang lowest.

Boys will be Men.

The Brains of a Fox will be of little Service, if you
play with the Paw of a Lion.

Bribes will enter without knocking.

A Bridle for the Tongue is a necessary Piece
of Furniture.

Bring not a Bagpipe to a Man in Trouble.

Broken Sacks will hold no Corn.

Burn not your House, to fright away the Mice.

Business and Action strengthen the Brain, but too much Study weakens it.

Busy-bodies never want a bad Day.

By Hook, or by Crook.

By Land or Water the Wind is ever in my Face.

By the Husk you may guess at the Nut.

Call me Cousin, but cozen me not.

Call your Husband Cuckold in Jest,
    and he'll ne'er suspect you.

A Calm is most welcome after a Storm.

Can a Mouse fall in Love with a Cat?

A careless Watch invites the vigilant Foe.

A Carper can cavil at any thing.

Carry Coals to *Newcastle*.

The Cart before the Horse.

Chance is a Dicer.

Charity begins at home, but should not end there.

Children and Fools tell Truth.

A close Mouth catcheth no Flies.

The Complaints of the present Times, is the general
Complaint of all Times.

A constant Guest is never welcome.

Content lodges oftner in Cottages than Palaces.

Count not your Chickens before they be hatch'd.

A covetous Man does nothing that he should do,
till he dies.

Covetousness is always filling a bottomless Vessel.

Craft must have Clothes; but Truth loves to go naked.

Cringing is a gainful Accomplishment.

A Crowd is not Company.

A Young Woman married to an old Man,
must behave like an old Woman.

A Danger foreseen is half avoided.

A Day to come shews longer than
a Year that's gone.

Dead Folks are past fooling.

Dead Folks can't bite.

Deceit is in Haste; but Honesty can
stay a fair Leisure.

Deeds are Fruits, Words are Leaves.

A Deluge of Words, and a Drop of Sense.

Despair hath damn'd some; but
Presumption Multitudes.

Destiny leads the willing, but drags the unwilling.

The Devil gets up to the Belfry, by the Vicar's Skirts.

Dexterity comes by Experience.

Do as little as you can to repent of.

Do nothing hastily, but catching of Fleas.

Don't turn Baker, if your Head be made of Butter.

Dress up even a little Toad, and it will look pretty.

Drink Wine, and have the Gout; drink none,
and have it too.

Drive that Nail that will go.

A Duck will not always dabble in the same Gutter.

Early ripe, early rotten.

Early sow, early mow.

Eat Peas with the King, and Cherries with the Beggar.

Education begins a Gentleman, Conversation
compleats him.

An Emmet may work its Heart out, but can
never make Honey.

Enquire not what boils in another's Pot.

The Epicure puts his Purse into his Belly; and
the Miser his Belly into his Purse.

Eternity has no grey Hairs.

Even Fools sometimes speak shrewdly.

Every...

...Age confutes old Errors, and begets new.

...Ass loves to hear himself bray.

...Dog has its day; and every Man his Hour.

...Dog is stout at his own Door.

...Man is a Fool, or a Physician, at Forty.

...Man must eat a Peck of Dirt before he dies.

...Man's nose will not make a Shooing-Horn.

...Path hath a Puddle.

...Slip is not a Fall.

...thing hath an end; and a Pudding hath two.

...Tub must stand upon its own Bottom.

Gone is the Goose that the great Egg did lay.

Gain got by a Lye, will burn one's Fingers.

A Gentleman without an Estate, is
a Pudding without Suet.

Getting out well, is a Quarter of the Journey.

Give a Dog an ill Name, and his Work is done.

Give even the Devil his Due.

Give him an Inch, and he'll take an Ell.

Give him but Rope enough, and he'll hang himself.

Give not Pearls to the Hogs.

Give the Piper a Penny to play, and Two-pence
to leave off.

Go into the Country, to hear what News in Town.

God help the Rich; the Poor can beg.

Gnomologia

God send you more Wit, and me more Money.

The golden Age never was the present Age.

Gone is the Goose that the great Egg did lay.

Good and Evil are chiefly in the Imagination.

A good archer is not known by his Arrows,
but his Aim.

Good Deeds remain; all things else perish.

A good Dog deserves a good Bone.

A good Friend is my nearest Relation.

A good Garden may have some Weeds.

Good Luck reaches farther than long Arms.

A good Marksman may miss.

A good Season for Courtship is, when the Widow
returns from the Funeral.

Good Words cost no more than bad.

Good Works will never save you; but you can never
be saved without them.

A Goose-Quill is more dangerous than a Lion's Claw.

A Grain of Prudence is worth a Pound of Craft.

Grasp no more than thy Hand will hold.

Gratitude is the least of Virtues, but Ingratitude
is the worst of Vices.

A great Blockhead hath not Stuff enough to make
a Man of Sense.

Great Braggers, little Doers.

A great Ceremony for a small Saint.

A great Fortune, in the Hands of a Fool,
is a great Misfortune.

Great Guts, and small Hopes.

A great Head, and a little Wit.

Great Minds and great Fortunes don't always
go together.

Great Ships ask deep Waters.

Great Wealth and Content, seldom live together.

Great Weight may hang on small Wires.

The greatest Oaks have been little Acorns.

A green Winter makes a fat Church yard.

Grief pent up will burst the Heart.

Half-witted Fellows speak much, and say little.

A Handsaw is a good thing, but not to shave with.

Hang not all your Bells upon one Horse.

Happiness generally depends more on the Opinion we have of Things, than on the Things themselves.

Happy is he, who hath sow'd his wild Oats betimes.

Harvest comes not every Day, tho' it come every Year.

Haste trips up its own Heels.

Hasty Glory goes out in a Snuff.

Have a Care of a silent Dog, and a still Water.

He...

...bought the Fox-skin for Three-pence, and sold
the Tail for a Shilling.

...builds Cages fit for Oxen, to keep Birds in.

...did me as much Good, as if he had piss'd
in my Pottage.

...does not believe, that does not live according
to his Belief.

...doth much, that doth a thing well.

...drags his Chain, and yet says, 'tis others that are mad.

...frets like gum'd Taffety.

...had better put his Horns in his Pocket
than blow them.

...had need of a long Spoon, that sups with the Devil.

...has a Head as big as a Horse, and Brains as much
as an Ass.

He...

...has a Mouth for every Matter.

...hath a good Judgment, that relieth not wholly
on his own.

...hath profited well, that likes *Cicero* well.

...hath ty'd a Knot with his Tongue, that he cannot
untie with all his Teeth.

...is as much out of his Element, as an Eel
in a Sand-bag.

...is good as long as he's pleas'd; and so is the Devil.

...is handsome that handsome doth.

...is like a Bell, that will go for every one that pulls it.

...is never alone, who is accompanied with
noble Thoughts.

...is not laughed at, that laughs at himself first.

...is one that will not lose his Cap in a Crowd.

...is rich that is satisfied.

...is sillier than a Crab, that has all his Brains
in his Belly.

...knows which Side of his Bread is butter'd.

...lights his Candle at both Ends.

...lives longest, that is awake most Hours.

...liveth long, that liveth well.

...put a fine Feather in his Cap.

...set my House afire, only to roast his Eggs.

He that's afraid of every Nettle, must not piss
in the Grass.

He who greases his Wheels, helps his Oxen.

He who is born a Fool, is never cured.

He who shareth Honey with a Bear, hath
the least Part of it.

Take me upon your Back,
and you'll know what I weigh.

He that...

...bites on every Weed, may light on Poison.

...bringeth a Present, findeth the Door open.

...can read and meditate, need not think the Evenings long, or Life tedious.

...ceaseth to be a Friend, never was a good one.

...cheateth in small things, is a Fool; but in great things, is a Rogue.

...contemplates on his Bed, hath a Day without a Night.

...falls to-day, may be up again to-morrow.

...feareth every Bush, must never go a Birding.

...gives his Heart, will not deny his Money.

...goes to Church with Brothers-in-Law, comes back without Kindred.

...grasps at too much, holds nothing fast.

...has feather'd his Nest, may fly when he will.

...has a great Nose, thinks every Body is speaking of it.

He that...

...has no Fools, Knaves, nor Beggars in his Family,
was begot by a Flash of Lightning.

...has no Silver in his Purse, should have Silver
on his Tongue.

...has too little, wants Wings to fly; he that has
too much, is incumbred with his large Tail.

...hath a Head of Wax, must not walk in the Sun.

...is busy, is tempted but by one Devil; he that is idle,
by a Legion.

...licks Honey from a Nettle, pays too dear for it.

...lies down with the Dogs, must rise with the Fleas.

...mindeth not his own Business, shall never
be trusted with mine.

...pays last, never pays twice.

...plants Trees, loves others besides himself.

...praiseth, bestows a Favour; he that detracts,
commits a Robbery.

...pryeth into the Clouds, may be struck with
a Thunderbolt.

...puts on a publick Gown, must put off a private
Person.

...refuses Praise the first Time, does it, because he
would have it the second.

...seeketh Trouble, never misseth of it.

...sows Thistles, shall reap Prickles.

...strikes my Dog, would strike me, if he durst.

...stumbles twice at the same Stone, deserves to have
his Shins broke.

...tells his Wife, is but lately married.

...ties up another Man's Dog, shall have nothing
left him but the Line.

...travels much, knows much.

...will enter Paradise, must come with a right Key.

...would know what shall be, must consider
what hath been.

He who wants Content, can't find an easy Chair.

He will shoot higher, that shoots at the Moon, than he that shoots at a Dunghil, tho' he miss the Mark.

The Head gray, and no Brains yet.

Health is great Riches.

Hedgehogs lodge among Thorns, because themselves are prickly.

Hell and Chancery are always open.

He's a Blockhead, that can't make two Verses; and he's a Fool, that makes four.

He's as brisk as Bottled Ale.

He's as sharp, as if he liv'd upon *Tewksbury* Mustard.

He's a Friend at a Sneeze; the most you can get of him, is a *God bless you.*

He's like a Bagpipe; you never hear him till his Belly is full.

High Places have their Precipices.

The higher the Hill, the lower the Grass.

Is it an Emperor's Business to catch Flies?

His Lungs are very sensible; for every thing makes
them laugh.

A Hog in Armour is still but a Hog.

Hold fast an Eel with a Fig-Leaf.

Hold your Tongue, Husband; let me talk, that
have all the Wit.

Home is home, be it never so homely.

Honest Men and Knaves may possibly wear
the same Cloth.

Honesty is the best Policy.

Hopes and Fears chequer Humane Life.

Hot Love is soon cold.

An Hour may destroy what an Age was a building.

How can the Cat help it, if the Maid be a Fool?

How difficult a thing it is, to persuade most Men
to be happy!

Hunger finds no Fault with the Cookery.

I will...

...either win the Horse, or lose the Saddle.

...keep no Cats, that will not catch Mice.

...not buy a Pig in a Poke.

...not keep a Dog, and bark my self.

...not play my Ace of Trumps yet.

...send him away with a Flea in his Ear.

...stick in your Skirts for this.

...watch your Water-Gate.

I cannot run and sit still, at the same time.

I deny that with both my Hands, and all my Teeth.

I have more to do, than a Dish to wash.

I have other Fish to fry.

I know enough to hold my Tongue, but not to speak.

I like writing with a Peacock's Quill; because its
Feathers are all Eyes.

I live; and Lords do no more.

I love you well, but touch not my Pocket.

I would have the Fruit, not the Basket.

I would not have your Cackling, for your Eggs.

An idle Person is the Devil's Playfellow.

An ill Cook should have a good Cleaver.

In the coldest Flint, there is hot Fire.

Industry is Fortune's right Hand, and Frugality her left.

Innovations are dangerous.

Is it an Emperor's Business to catch Flies?

If...

...any Fool finds the Cap fit him, let him wear it.

...any thing stay, let Work stay.

...ever I catch his Cart overthrowing, I'll give it one shove.

...the Frog and Mouse quarrel, the Kite will see them agreed.

...I am a Fool, put you your Finger in my Mouth.

...it were a Bear, it would bite you.

...it were not for the Belly, the Back might wear Gold.

...*Jack's* in Love, he's no Judge of *Jill's* Beauty.

...Marriages are made in Heaven, you had few Friends there.

...Money be not thy Servant, it will be thy Master.

...the Mountain will not come to *Mahomet*, *Mahomet* must go to the Mountain.

If...

...one, two, or three tell you, you are an Ass,
put on a Tail.

...the Sky fall, we shall catch Larks.

...Strokes are good to give, they are good to receive.

...thy Hand be in a Lion's Mouth, get it out as fast
as thou can'st.

...to-day will not, to-morrow may.

...Virtue keep Court within, Honour will attend without.

...we are bound to forgive an Enemy, we are not bound
to trust him.

...we did not flatter our selves, no Body else could.

...a Word be worth a Shilling, Silence is worth two.

...you be a Fool, and I be a Fool, there will be
no meddling with us.

...you buy the Cow, take the Tail into the Bargain.

...you had as little Money as Manners,
you'd be the poorest of all your Kin.

...you have many Irons in the Fire, some will burn.

...you increase the Water, you must increase the Malt.

...you leap into a Well, Providence is not bound
to fetch you out.

...you run after two Hares, you will catch neither.

...you sleep till Noon, you have no right to complain
that the Days are short.

...you will obtain, you must attempt.

...you would have a Hen lay, you must bear with
her cackling.

...your Head be Glass, engage not at throwing Stones.

...your Luck goes on at this Rate, you may very well
hope to be hang'd.

Rob Peter, to pay Paul.

It is...

...as long a Coming, as *Cotswold* Barley.

...at Courts, as it is in Ponds; some Fish, some Frogs.

...better to have a Hen to Morrow, than an Egg to Day.

...better to pay, and have but little left; than to have much, and be always in Debt.

...better to spin all Night with *Penelope*, than sing with *Helen* all Day.

...even as broad as it is long.

...for want of thinking, that most Men are undone.

...good sheltering under an old Hedge.

...good to have a Hatch before one's Door.

...good to have two Strings to one's Bow.

...a great Point of Wisdom, to find out one's own Folly.

...hard to be high and humble.

...hard to shave an Egg.

...humane to err, but diabolical to persevere.

It is...

...in vain to mislike the current Fashion.

...like Nuts to an Ape.

...Madness to put on Gloves, when you are stark naked.

...no good Hen, that cackles in your House, and
lays in another's.

...not every one that can pickle well.

...not the Cowl, that makes the Frier.

...not lost, if it comes at last.

...the ordinary way of the World, to keep Folly at
the Helm, and Wisdom under the Hatches.

...safe taking a slice off a Cut Loaf.

...a Sign of a worthy Spirit, whom Honour amends.

...a silly Fish, that is caught twice with the same Bait.

...a silly Goose, that comes to a Foxe's Sermon.

...a Sin against Hospitality, to open your Doors, and
shut up your Countenance.

...sooner said than done.

Laws catch Flies, but let the Hornets go free.

Learning makes a Man fit Company for himself.

Less of your Courtship, I pray, and more of your Coin.

Let not another shuffle and cut the Cards thou art
to deal out.

Let not thy Tongue run away with thy Brains.

Life is half spent, before we know what it is.

Like a Cat, he'll still fall upon his Legs.

Like a Collier's Sack; bad without, but worse within.

Like the Gardener's Dog; that neither eats Cabbage
himself, nor lets any Body else.

Like the Smith's Dog; that sleeps at the noise of
the Hammers, and wakes at the crashing of Teeth.

A little Debt makes a Debtor, but a great one
an Enemy.

Little Sticks kindle a Fire; but great ones put it out.

A little Time may be enough to hatch a great deal
of Mischief.

Live, and let live.

London-Bridge was made for Wise Men to pass over,
and for Fools to pass under.

Long e're you cut down an Oak with a Pen-knife.

Look high, and fall low.

Look not a given Horse in the Mouth.

Loquacity is the Fistula of the Soul, ever running,
and never cur'd.

Love comes in at the Window, and flies out
at the Door.

Love does much; but Money does more.

a Mouse must not think to cast a Shadow
like an Elephant.

Love, the Itch, and a Cough cannot be hid.

Love me little, and love me long.

Love me, love my Dog.

A low Hedge is easily leap'd over.

A Lye has no Leg, but a Scandal has Wings.

A Lyon may come to be beholding to a Mouse.

Madam, I am to the utmost of my Power, not yours.

Maids, make much of one; good Men are scarce.

Make the best of a bad Bargain.

Make Hay, while the Sun shines.

Make not thy Sail too big for the Ballast.

Make not thy Tail broader than thy Wings.

Make a Virtue of Necessity.

Make the young one squeak, and you'll catch
the old one.

Malice drinketh up the greatest Part of its own Poison.

Man had perish'd long ago, had it not been for publick
spirited Persons.

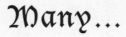

Many...

...can pack the Cards better than they can play.

...come to bring their Clothes to Church rather than themselves.

...drops of Water, will sink a Ship.

...get into a Dispute well, that cannot get out well.

...Hands make light Work.

...make strait Things crooked, but few the contrary.

...rise under their Burthens, more like Camels, than Palm-Trees.

...talk like Philosophers, and live like Fools.

...that are Wits in jest, are Fools in earnest.

...that go out for Wool, come home shorn.

...Things grow in the Garden, that were never sow'd there.

...would be Cowards if they had Courage enough.

The Man in the Moon drinks Claret.

A Man, like a Watch, is to be valued for his Goings.

A Man may be young in Years, and yet old in Hours.

A Man may come to Market, tho' he don't buy Oysters.

A Man may lead his Horse to Water, but cannot make him drink.

A Man may provoke his own Dog to bite him.

Man punishes the Action, but God the Intention.

A Man that keeps Riches, and enjoys them not, is like an Ass that carries Gold and eats Thistles.

Marriage and Hanging go by Destiny.

Marriage leapeth up upon the Saddle, and soon after Repentance upon the Crupper.

Men of Business must not break their Word twice.

The Mind is the Man.

Mirth and Motion prolong Life.

Out of the Frying-pan into the Fire.

Mischief comes by the Pound, and goes away
by the Ounce.

Misfortunes tell us, what Fortune is.

Money is a Sword, that can cut even the *Gordian* Knot.

Money is too inconsiderable to love; yet too useful
to throw away.

The Moon is made of green Cheese.

The more Cooks, the worse Broth.

More Flies are taken with a Drop of Honey than
a Tun of Vinegar.

The more Laws, the more Offenders.

Mortal Man must not keep up immortal Anger.

A Mouse must not think to cast a Shadow
like an Elephant.

Mouth-Civility is no great Pains, but may turn
to good Account.

Much would have more; but often meets with less.

Must I tell you a Tale, and find you Ears too?

Mustard is good Sauce, but Mirth is better.

My Dame fed her Hens with meer Thanks,
and they laid no Eggs.

My House is my Castle.

My Mind to me a Kingdom is.

My Money comes in at the Door, and flies out
at the Window.

My Teeth are nearer to me than my Kindred is.

Natural Folly is bad enough; but learned Folly
is intolerable.

Nay, stay, quoth *Stringer*, when his Neck was
in the Halter.

Never chuse Linen nor Women by Candle-Light.

Never rub your Eye but with your Elbow.

Never too old to learn what is good.

New Brooms sweep clean.

Night is the Mother of Thought.

A Nightingale cannot sing in a Cage.

None but Cats and Dogs are allowed to quarrel
in my House.

No...

...Condition so low, but may have Hopes;
none so high, but may have Fears.

...Day passeth, without something we wish not.

...Dish pleases all Palates alike.

...Fool like the old Fool.

...good building without a good Foundation.

...Man is his Craft's Master the first Day.

...Man was ever scared into Heaven.

...Man was made for Sports and Recreations.

...Merchant gets always.

...Rose without a Prickle.

...Smoak without some Fire.

...Sweet, without some Sweat.

...Sweetness in a Cabbage twice boil'd, nor in a
Tale twice told.

...Tyrant can take from you your Knowledge
and Wisdom.

...Vice goes alone.

None, but a wise Man, can employ Leisure well.

None knows what will happen to him before Sunset.

None knows the Weight of another's Burthen.

None so deaf, as he that will not hear.

Not to hear Conscience, is the Way to silence it.

Nothing costs so much as what is given us.

Nothing is ours, but Time.

Nothing venture, nothing have.

Nothing's impossible to a willing Mind.

Nothing's more playful than a young cat, nor more
grave than the old One.

Now-a-days Truth is the greatest News.

Offer not the Pear to him that gave the Apple.

Old Age is not so fiery as Youth; but when once provoked, cannot be appeased.

Old Foxes want no Tutors.

An old wrinkle never wears out.

An open Door may tempt a Saint.

An Ounce of Fortune is worth a Pound of Forecast.

An Ounce of Wisdom is worth a Pound of Wit.

Out of the Frying-pan into the Fire.

Out of Sight; out of Mind.

a good Dog deserves a good Bone.

One...

...barking Dog, sets all the Street a barking.

...Bird in the Hand, is worth two in the Bush.

...Eye-witness is better than ten Hearsays.

...good Turn deserves another.

...had better forgive a Debt, where he cannot recover
so much as his Charges.

...Hand may wash the other, but both the Face.

...Hour's sleep before Midnight, is worth two after.

...may point at a Star, but not pull at it.

...Suit of Law breeds twenty.

...Thing thinketh the Horse, and another
he that saddles him.

Parents are Patterns.

The Parings of a Pippin are better than a whole Crab.

The Passions are like Fire and Water; good Servants,
but bad Masters.

Patience is good for abundance of Things besides
the Gout.

Patience, Money, and Time, bring all Things to pass.

A Penny more buys the Whistle.

A Penny sav'd is Two-pence got.

Penny-wise, and Pound-foolish.

A Pilot is not chosen for his Riches, but his Knowledge.

Popular Opinion is the greatest Lie in the World.

Possession is eleven Points in the Law.

Possibilities are infinite.

A Pot that belongs to many, is ill stirr'd and
worse boil'd.

Praise is pleasing to him that thinks he deserves it.

Precious Things are not found in Heaps.

Prevention is much preferable to Cure.

Pride is as loud a Beggar as Want; and a great deal
more saucy.

Pride seldom leaves its Master without a Fall.

Promises may get Friends, but 'tis Performances
that keep them.

The Proof of a Pudding is in the eating.

Prosperity gets Followers; but Adversity
distinguishes them.

Providence directs the Dice.

A Puff of Wind and the Praise of the People,
weigh alike.

As innocent as a Devil of two Years old.

The Race is got by running.

Raise up no Spirits, that you cannot conjure
down again.

Rashness may conquer; but it's not likely it should.

Raw Leather will stretch.

A ready Way to lose your Friend, is to lend him Money.

Rebukes ought not to have a Grain of Salt more
than of Sugar.

Rejoice, Shrovetide, to-day; for to-morrow
you'll be Ashes.

Repetition is every where unacceptable,
tho' 'twere in *Homer*.

Revenge never repairs an Injury.

Riches abuse them, who know not how to use them.

Riches are but the Baggage of Fortune.

Riches have made more covetous Men, than
Covetousness hath made rich Men.

Rob *Peter,* to pay *Paul.*

A Rogue's Wardrobe is Harbour for a Louse.

Rolling Stones gather no Moss.

Rome was not built in a Day.

A Rope and Butter; if one slip, t'other will hold.

Sacrifice not thy Heart upon every altar.

Sadness and Gladness succeed each other.

Salt spilt, is seldom clean taken up.

Satires run faster than Panegyricks.

Say not ill of the Year, till it be past.

Scratching is bad; because it begins with Pleasure,
and ends with Pain.

Seeing's Believing, but Feeling's the Truth.

Seek not to reform every one's Dial by your Watch.

Seek, till you find; and you'll not lose your Labour.

Send not for an Hatchet, to break open an Egg with.

Gnomologia

Set not your House on Fire, to be reveng'd
of the Moon.

Shake a *Leicestershire*-Man by the Collar, and you shall
hear the Beans rattle in his Belly.

She, that hath Spice enough, may season as she likes.

Shew me a Liar, and I'll shew you a Thief.

Short and sweet.

Sickness tells us what we are.

The Singing-man keeps his Shop in his throat.

Sins and Debts are always more than we think
them to be.

A Slip of the Foot may be soon recover'd; but that
of the Tongue perhaps never.

A small Leak will sink a great Ship.

Small Pitchers have wide Ears.

Soft Words break no Bones.

Solitude make us love our selves; Conversation, others.

Some are Atheists only in fair Weather.

Some have been thought brave, because they were afraid to run away.

Some Wits can digest, before others can chew.

Sometimes it costs a great deal to do Mischief.

Sorrow comes unsent for.

The Soul is not where it lives, but where it loves.

Sour Grapes can ne'er make sweet Wine.

Spare the Rod, and spoil the Child.

Spare your Rhetoric, and speak Logic.

A Sparrow in Hand is worth a Pheasant that flyeth by.

A Spur in the Head is worth two in the Heels.

Standers-by see more than the Gamesters.

Step after Step, the Ladder is ascended.

Gnomologia

The Sting of a Reproach is the Truth of it.

The Stone, that lieth not in your way, need
not offend you.

A stout Heart crushes ill Luck.

A streight Stick is crooked in the Water.

Strike, while the Iron is hot.

A Stumble may prevent a Fall.

Such a Father, such a Son.

Such a Reason pissed my Goose.

Suffering for a Friend, doubleth the Friendship.

The Sun can be seen by nothing but its own Light.

The Sun has stood still, but Time never did.

Surgeons must have an Eagle's Eye, a Lion's Heart,
and a Lady's Hand.

Suspicion may be no Fault, but shewing it may
be a great one.

An Ass is but an Ass, tho' laden with Gold.

Tailors and Writers must mind the Fashion.

Take all, and pay the Baker.

Take an Hair of the same Dog that bit you.

Take away my good Name, and take away my Life.

Take Courage; younger than thou have been hanged.

Take hold of a good Minute.

Take me upon your Back, and you'll know
what I weigh.

Take Time, while Time is; for Time will away.

Teaching of others, teacheth the Teacher.

Tell a Tale to a Mare, and she'll let a Fart.

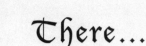

There...

...are more natural Buffoons, than artificial.

...are more Ways to the Wood than one.

...is as much hold of his Words, as of a wet Eel's Tail.

...is a Bone for you to pick.

...is a critical Minute for all Things.

...is a Fault in the House, but would you have it
built without any?

...is a Snake in the Grass.

...is no adding to Fundamentals.

...is no better Looking-Glass than an old Friend.

...is no going to Heaven in a Sedan.

...may be Blue, and better Blue.

Gnomologia

That Hour is coming, when we shall more earnestly
wish to gain Time, than ever we studied to spend it.

That is as likely as to see an Hog fly.

That is as true as that the Cat crew, and the
Cock rock'd the Cradle.

That is no easy Pill to be swallowed.

That is well spoken, which is well taken.

That was new, in last Year's new Almanack.

That, which will not be Butter, must be
made into Cheese.

That, which you sow, you must reap.

Things hardly attain'd, are long retain'd.

A thinking Man is always striking out something new.

This Day is yours, but whose shall To-morrow be?

This World is ever running its round.

Tho' all Men were made of one Metal, yet they were
not cast all in the same Mould.

Tho' the Fox runs, the Chickens have Wings.

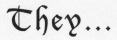

They...

...agree like Bells; they want nothing but hanging.

...agree like *London* Clocks.

...are Clove and Orange.

...are Finger and Thumb.

...are Hand and Glove.

...are rich, who have true Friends.

...that have good store of Butter, may lay it on thick.

...that walk in the Sun, must be content to be tan'd.

...were both equally bad; so the Devil put
them together.

Gnomologia

Tho' the Heavens be glorious, yet they are not all Stars.

Tho' you are bound to love your Enemy, you are not
bound to put your Sword in his Hand.

Those, that make the best Use of their Time,
have none to spare.

Thou art as like to obtain thy Wish, as the Wolf is
to eat the Moon.

Thou shalt have Moon-shine in thy Mustard-Pot for it.

The Thought has good Wings, and the Quill
a good Tongue.

A thousand Years hence, the River will run as it did.

Three may keep Counsel, if two be away.

Thrift is the Philosopher's Stone.

Time and Tide tarry for no Man.

Time is the Rider that breaks in Youth.

A tired Traveller must be glad of an Ass,
if he have not an Horse.

'Tis...

...the early Bird, that catcheth the Worm.

...easier to avoid a Fault, than acquire Perfection.

...easier to know how to speak, than how to be silent.

...easier to miss, than to hit a Needle's Eye.

...easier to preserve a Friend, than to recover him when lost.

...easy to fall into a Trap; but hard to get out again.

...harder to unlearn than learn.

...in vain to speak Reason, where 'twill not be heard.

...Liberty, that every one loves.

...not the Beard, that makes the Philosopher.

...not every Question, that deserves an Answer.

...not for every one to catch a Salmon.

...not the Habit, that makes the Monk.

...not the Matter, but the Mind.

...Perseverance that prevails.

...Pity thou art not a little more Tongue-tied.

...Wisdom sometimes to seem a Fool.

To-Day is Yesterday's Pupil.

To-Day me, To-Morrow thee.

Too great and sudden Changes, tho' for the better,
are not easily born.

Too much consulting confounds.

Too much Familiarity breeds Contempt.

Too much Scratching, pains; too much Talking, plagues.

To...

...eat, and to scratch, a Man need but begin.

...fly with waxed Wings.

...go as fast as a Friar, that is invited to Dinner.

...hit the Nail on the Head.

...hold one's Nose to the Grind-stone.

...hold with the Hare, and run with the Hounds.

...kill two Birds with one Stone.

...leave all at Sixes and Sevens.

...leave no Stone unturn'd.

...make a Mountain of a Mole-hill.

...put new Handles to an old Pot.

...run the Wild-Goose Chace.

...see may be easy; but to foresee, that is
the fine Thing.

...seek a Needle in a Bottle of Hay.

...serve the People, is worse than to serve two Masters.

...talk without thinking, is to shoot without aiming.

...wear a Horn, and not know it, will do one no more
Harm, than to eat a Fly and not see it.

...whisper Proclamations is ridiculous.

Troy was not took in a Day.

True Blue will never stain.

A true Reformation must begin at the upper End.

Trust him no further than you can throw him.

Two Anons, and a By and By, are an Hour and a half.

'Twould make one Scratch, where it doth not itch.

Count not your Chickens before they be hatch'd.

An unbounded Liberty will undo us.

Unmannerly a little, is better than troublesome
a great deal.

Use Pastime, so as not to lose Time.

The usefullest Truths are the plainest.

Valour would fight, but Discretion would run away.

Vanity will prove Vexation.

Varnishing hides a Crack.

Venture a small Fish to catch a great one.

A very good or very bad Poet is remarkable; but
a middling one, who can bear?

Vice would be frightful, if it did not wear a Mask.

Virtue and Happiness are but two Names for
the same Thing.

Virtue dwells not in the Tongue, but in the Heart.

Virtue hath few *Platonick* Lovers.

Virtue may be overclouded a while, but 'twill shine
at the last.

We...

...are all *Adam's* Children; but Silk makes
the Difference.

...are apt to believe what we wish for.

...are ever young enough to Sin; never old enough
to repent.

...desire but one Feather out of your Goose.

...easily forget our Faults, when no body knows them.

...must not look for a Golden Life in an Iron Age.

...should play, to live; not live, to play.

A Wager is a Fool's Argument.

The Way to live much, is to begin to live well betimes.

Well lather'd is half shaven.

A wet Hand will hold a dead Herring.

What avails it me, to draw one Foot out of the Mire, and stick the other in?

What Children hear at Home, soon flies abroad.

What the good Wife spares, the Cat eats.

What the Heart thinketh, the Tongue speaketh.

What may be done at any Time, will be done at no Time.

What should a Cow do with a Nutmeg?

Where the River is deepest, it runneth quietest.

Where the Will is ready, the Feet are light.

Who ever repented of a good Action?

Who hath Horns in his Bosom, let him not put them on his Forehead.

When...

...the Cat's gone, the Mice grow sawcy.

...*Dover* and *Calais* meet.

...the Eye sees what it never saw, the Heart will think
what it never thought.

...Flatterers meet, the Devil goes to Dinner.

...Fortune smiles, embrace her.

...the Head aketh, all the Body feels it.

...the Heart is a fire, some Sparks will fly out
of the Mouth.

...Passion entereth at the Fore-gate, Wisdom goeth out
of the Postern.

...the Rights of Hospitality are invaded, Revenge
is almost allowable.

...Sorrow is asleep, wake it not.

...a Tree is once a falling, every one cries, down with it.

...two Knaves deal, the Devil drives the Bargain.

...War beginneth, Hell openeth.

...the Wine is in, the Wit is out.

...Wine sinks, Words swim.

Who marrieth for Love without Money, hath merry
Nights and sorry Days.

Who more busy than they that have least to do?

Who never climbed high, never fell low.

Who robs a *Cambridge*-Scholar, robs twenty.

Who'd keep a Cow, when he may have a Quart
of Milk for a Penny?

The whole Ocean is made up of single Drops.

A wicked Book is the wickeder, because
it cannot repent.

A wicked Companion invites us all to Hell.

Wilful Waste brings woful Want.

A willing Mind makes a light Foot.

Wind and Weather, do your utmost.

Wisdom don't always speak in *Greek* and *Latin*.

Wisdom is a good Purchase, tho' we pay dear for it.

A wise Head hath a close Mouth to it.

Can a Mouse fall in Love with a Cat?

Gnomologia

A wise Man begins in the End; a Fool ends
in the Beginning.

A wise Man's Thoughts walk within him, but a Fool's
without him.

Wise Men make Proverbs, and Fools repeat them.

Wit and Wisdom are like the seven Stars;
seldom seen together.

The Wit of you, and the Wool of a blue Dog,
would make a very good Medley.

Wit without Wisdom, cuts other Men's Meat and
its own Fingers.

With Foxes we must play the Fox.

With-hold not thy Money, where there is Need;
and waste it not, where there is none.

Wolves may lose their Teeth, but not their Nature.

Women's Work is never done.

A Word and a Stone let go, cannot be called back.

A Word spoke, is an Arrow let fly.

A Word to the Wise.

The World is a Net, the more we stir in it, the more we are entangled.

The World would perish, were all Men learned.

Worth hath been under-rated, ever since Wealth hath been over-valued.

Would you dye a Raven black?

Would you thatch your House with Pancakes?

Wounds may heal; but not those, that are made by ill Words.

Wrinkled Purses make wrinkled Faces.

Write with the Learned, but speak with the Vulgar.

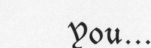

you...

...are an honest Man, and I am your Uncle; and that's two Lies.

...are a Man among the Geese, when the Gander is away.

...can't drive a Wind-Mill with a Pair of Bellows.

...can't eat your Cake, and have it too.

...gaz'd at the Moon, and fell in the Gutter.

...have good Manners, but never carry them about you.

...have made a Hand of it, like a Foot.

...may follow him long, e're a Shilling drop from him.

...may truss up all his Wit in an Eggshell.

...must be content sometimes with rough Roads.

...must look where it is not, as well as where it is.

...must not cut and deal too.

...shall never beat the Fly from the Candle,
tho' she burn for it.

...shall never clap a Padlock upon my Tongue.

...should ask the World's Leave, before you commend
your self.

...shut your Budget, before it's full.

...sift Night and Day, and get nothing but Bran.

...starve in a Cook's Shop.

...take me up, before I'm down.

...take more Care of your Shoe, than your Foot.

...to the Cabbage, and I to the Beef.

...were born, when Wit was scarce.

...were bred in *Brazen-Nose* College.

...will never repent of being Patient and Sober.

Gnomologia

You'll be good, when your Goose pisseth.

You'll keep it no longer, than you can
a Cat in a Wheel-barrow.

You'll never be Mad, you are of so many Minds.

Young Men are made Wise; old Men become so.

A young Prodigal, an old Mumper.

Young Tongue is made of very loose Leather.

A young Twig is easier twisted than an old Tree.

A Young Woman married to an old Man,
must behave like an old Woman.

Your Bread is butter'd on both Sides.

Your Wits are gone a Wool-gathering.

Youth and white Paper take any Impression.

A wet Hand will hold a dead Herring.

Zeal is by no Means the same with Fury and Rage.

Zeal without Knowledge is Fire without Light.

finis

A *short Account of the* LIBRARY.

THE Library-Company was form'd in 1731, by Conftitutions or Articles entred into by 50 Perfons, each obliging himfelf to pay 40 s. for purchafing the firft Parcel of Books, and 10 s. *per annum* to defray Charges and encreafe the Library.

Ten Directors or Managers of the Library, and a Treafurer, are chofen yearly by Vote, at a General Meeting of the Company.

The Number of Members are now encreafed to upwards of 70. Perfons enclining to be admitted, apply to any one of the Directors, who nominates them at the next monthly Meeting of Directors; and being allowed, and paying to the Treafurer the Value of a Share at the Time, and figning the Articles, they become Members.

Any Member may borrow a Book for 2, 3, or 4 Weeks, leaving his Note for double Value, and paying a fmall Penalty if 'tis not return'd at the Time agreed; which Penalties are applied to defraying Charges, or purchafing more Books.

Every Member has an abfolute Property in his Share; may devife it in his Will, or difpofe of it when he pleafes to any Perfon the Directors approve. And Shares fo fold have always hitherto yielded as much as they had coft. As Shares encreafe yearly in Value 10 s. fo much being yearly added by each Subfcriber to the Stock of Books, a Share which at firft was worth but 40 s. is now valued at 6 l. 10 s. But for this fmall Sum, which laid out in Books, would go but a little Way, every Member has the Ufe of a Library now worth upwards of 500 l. whereby *Knowledge* is in this City render'd more cheap and eafy to be come at, to the great Pleafure and Advantage of the ftudious Part of the Inhabitants.

Thofe who are not Subfcribers may notwithftanding borrow Books, leaving in the Hands of the Librarian, as a Pledge, a Sum of Money proportion'd to the Value of the Book borrow'd, and paying a fmall Acknowledgment for the Reading, which is apply'd to the Ufe of the Library.

The Library is open and Attendance given every Saturday Afternoon from 4 a Clock 'til 8.

Befides the Books in this Catalogue given to the Library, the Company have been favour'd with feveral generous Donations; as, a curious Air-Pump, with its Apparatus, a large double Microfcope, and other valuable Inftruments, from the Hon. JOHN PENN, Efq; A handfome Lot of Ground whereon to build a Houfe for the Library, from the Hon. THOMAS PENN, Efq; Proprietaries of the Province; and the Sum of 34 l. Sterl. (to be laid out in Books) from Dr. *Sydferfe*, late of *Antigua*.

At prefent the Books are depofited in the Weft Wing of the State-Houfe, by Favour of the General Affembly.

It is now Ten Years fince the Company was firft eftablifhed; and we have the Pleafure of obferving, That tho' 'tis compos'd of fo many Perfons of different Sects, Parties and Ways of Thinking, yet no Differences relating to the Affairs of the Library, have arifen among us; but every Thing has been conducted with great Harmony, and to general Satisfaction. Which happy Circumftance will, we hope, always continue.

Note, *A Copy of the Articles or Conftitutions is left in the Library, for the Perufal of all that defire to be more fully informed.*

Benjamin Franklin provided this account of the Library Company of Philadelphia in 1741. Ever the practical printer, he wrote it to fill a blank page at the end of the catalogue he published, itemizing the 375 titles then in the Library's collection.

The Library Company
of Philadelphia

'Benefits for the common good'

The original *Gnomologia* is just one of countless colonial treasures that constitute the holdings of the Library Company of Philadelphia, itself a national treasure.

Benjamin Franklin was its erstwhile founder. He had the idea that colonial Philadelphians needed a library, and the best way to obtain the books for it would be to make it a shareholder's library. And so on July 1, 1731, Franklin and a group of like-minded readers drew up the Articles of Agreement for what would become the first lending library in America.

Its motto was *Communiter Bona profundere Deum est:* "To pour forth benefits for the common good is divine." With typical Franklinesque practicality, the Library levied a modest annual subscription fee on each shareholder for the benefit of all, using the shillings to buy ever more books from abroad.

By 1741, the Library boasted 375 books that both members and nonmembers could borrow. (The latter were encouraged to pay "a small Acknowledgment for the Reading," although the collection of these Acknowledgments was delightfully lax.) By 1770, the Library housed 2,033 volumes.

Fittingly, given its independence-minded founder, the Library provided the venue for the 1774 meeting of the First

Continental Congress. It would also be a forerunner to the Library of Congress.

Today the Library Company of Philadelphia is a leading national research library, specializing in American culture and history from colonial days through 1900. It continues to operate for the benefit of the common good, preserving a young country's remarkable beginnings while expanding its holdings and providing research fellowships in Early American History and Culture. It is the only major library from colonial times to remain in existence and operation. Its doors are open to all, and all are invited to become members.

Those who cannot visit in person are invited to visit online at www.librarycompany.org.

Gratitude

"The heaviest debt is that of gratitude," Benjamin Franklin is reported to have said. We are indeed indebted to those who helped bring this book to fruition.

John C. Van Horne and James Green of the Library Company of Philadelphia graciously invited us to treasure-hunt in their archives and heroically entrusted us with the loan of their rare *Gnomologia*. Linda Wisniewski and Nicole Scalessa were our cheerful and ready sources for scans of various Library Company elements.

Our quest to have photographs taken of the original's fragile pages led us to the library of Florida Atlantic University (thanks to the suggestion of Norma Kane at the Delray Beach Public Library). Dr. William Miller and Dee Cael not only opened their doors to us but found two pairs of willing hands to painstakingly hold and photograph each page. To Salwa Ismail Patel and Heather Reitano, our thanks and admiration for the remarkable patience you had.

Janice Miller willingly found time to transcribe the pages in no time at all, and Tina St. Pierre checked them with her unerring eye.

They all prove the maxim that nothing succeeds like people who care—and deeply—about what they do.

Index of Key Words

N

O

P

wax 30, 76

wealth 23, 87

weather 66, 84

weed 6, 22, 29

weight 23, 55

whisper 77

wife 9, 31, 82

wind 10, 60, 84, 88

wine 15, 66, 83

wings 30, 46, 47, 71, 73, 76

winter 23

wisdom 2, 9, 41, 42, 54, 56, 75, 83, 84, 86

wise 6, 44, 55, 59, 84, 86, 87, 90

wish 54, 71, 73, 81

wit 5, 22, 23, 24, 34, 48, 56, 66, 83, 86, 88, 89, 90

woman 53, 86, 90

wood 70

wool 8, 48, 86, 90

word 7, 14, 22, 38, 49, 65, 70, 83, 86, 87

work 16, 21, 22, 37, 48, 86

world 2, 42, 59, 71, 87, 89

wrinkle 56, 87

Y

year 1, 4, 9, 14, 24, 49, 64, 71, 73

yesterday 75

youth 56, 73, 90

Z

zeal 92

a word spoke, is an arrow let fly.